Inspired by His Word
From the "WORD" Up! Collection

Author

Mary Hilton

Inspired by His Word

Copyright © 2017 Christ Inspired Words Ministry

All rights reserved. No part of this publication may be reproduced, stored in a retrieved system or transmitted in any form or by any means, without prior permission from the copyright owner.

Scripture quotations taken from the New American Standard Bible® (NASB),
Copyright © 1960, 1962, 1963, 1968, 1971, 1972, 1973, 1975, 1977, 1995 by The Lockman Foundation
Used by permission. www.Lockman.org

Scripture quotations taken from the Amplified® Bible (AMPC), Copyright © 1954, 1958, 1962, 1964, 1965, 1987 by The Lockman Foundation. Used by permission. www.Lockman.org

Scripture taken from the New King James Version®.
Copyright © 1982 by Thomas Nelson.
Used by permission. All rights reserved.

ISBN-13: 978-1978438163

THANK YOU

This Book is dedicated to all those readers and supporters of "WORD" Up! and Christ Inspired Words Ministry who have encouraged and supported me from its inception. You know who you are.

You all have questioned , pushed and prodded me about getting the book out for too many years past. So here it is!

I just want to say THANK YOU to you all.

Mostly I say THANK YOU to my Lord and Saviour JESUS CHRIST who died on the Cross for me so that I could be set free to be used by Him in different ways including bringing forth the "WORD" Up! series not only to bless others but mainly to bring glory to His Precious Name.

Preface

In 2005, I gave my life to Christ at the New Testament Church of God in Mile End East London after hearing the preaching of the Senior Pastor and feeling the conviction of the Holy Spirit that my life was not at all 'alright' as I had been tricked into believing it was. That summer Sunday morning in July changed the direction of my life forever.

From very soon afterwards, I discovered that I had been blessed with a creative writing gift. In fact, I had always loved writing stories as a young child and had good imagination. So God, in His infinite wisdom, really just revived what He had placed in me a long time ago, put His anointing on it and began to use it for His glory.

The '"WORD" Up!' collection comes out of a growing love for God's word. Verses of scripture would jump out of the page as I read and in my excitement I'd send them on with a few words of comment to four or five of my phone contacts saying how excited I was about the text. This started back in 2006. Today, the audience has grown share in my excitement each week and have for some years encouraged me to get a book together. So here it is. God has developed those short texts into what you are about to read in this book.

So I pray that as you dive into 'Inspired by His Word' not only will you be blessed, but that you will also be encouraged, challenged, and provoked. Most importantly, I pray that each page brings deeper enlightenment of the love that Christ Jesus has for you. If you know Him be inspired to know Him more. If you don't then I pray that 'Inspired By His Word' will incite you to *'taste and see that the Lord is good'.*

He awaits you.
Shalom

Mary Hilton
Author

Inspired By His Word

Inspired by His Word

CONTENTS

1 Spirit and Life
2 The Trumpet Warning
3 Enlarge My Territory
4 You Being Here is Not By Chance
5 The Power of the Word
6 The Shaken vs The Unshakeable
7 Do You Know How Valuable You Are?
8 Watch Out, Watch Out! The Heart is About
9 But What If He Doesn't?
10 Strength Like No Other
11 Don't Take Offence
12 Do You Really Want What You Pray For?
13 Don't You Recognise Me Anymore?
14 Good Trees Cant Bare Bad Fruit
15 The Blood He Shed, It Went Ahead
16 The Youth are Our Responsibility
17 Jesus, Our Sure and Steadfast Hope
18 Recognise the Idols in Your Heart

19	Living as a Doer
20	It's Yours! God Said It!
21	Prune Me Lord, Prune Me!
22	Be on Your Guard
23	Be Strong
24	What's That You're Saying?
25	What Are You Bringing?
26	Strange Instruction
27	Thank God for My Afflictions
28	Wait Patiently
29	Mind Control
30	Time for Change

Inspired by His Word

ACKNOWLEDGMENTS

I acknowledge all those authors who have stepped out of the boat and have pressed in with the gifts and the anointing which the Lord God has blessed them with and have in some way touched the lives of readers worldwide by being obedient.

Thank You for being examples to me of those whose dreams come to pass and will not be found in the graveyard of dreams.

Inspired By His Word

Inspired by His Word

Spirit and Life

Job 33:4 *'The Spirit of God has made me and the breath of the Almighty gives me life.'* (NASB)

The 'Spirit of God'!

Imagine that! The same Spirit of God which hovered above the earth when it was null and void. The same Spirit of God which came down on the young virgin girl Mary and filled her with the seed that brought forth the Lord Jesus Christ. The same Spirit of God that filled David and gave Him the power to overcome Goliath. The same Spirit of God that came upon Saul causing him to prophesy and be changed into another man. The same Spirit of God that came down and rested on the Apostles as they prayed in one accord in the Upper Room. It's that same Spirit of God which, as this verse says, has made us. It has made us. That Spirit of God which changes us into another person. It has made us! Without the Spirit of God working in us who would we be? What would our lives be?

Just take a breath for a moment and think about that. Think about that Spirit of God that has made you and which lives in you. Think about His power which has been deposited in you. It's a power beyond human comprehension. And as you take that breath, think for a moment about...that... breath (exhale).

Something we do, without thinking. Something we take for granted. Breath! The breath of the Almighty. His 'ruach'...the source of life that runs through us...pneuma, the breath of the Spirit. The breath of that same Spirit that made you, dwells in you and gives you life! Wow! Christ said *'I have come so that they might have life and have it more abundantly'*. We have that *'abundant life'* living in us.

The 'abundant life'. It's been breathed into us, the breath of the Almighty God. What an awesome awesome truth!

The Spirit of God has made me and the breath of the Almighty gives me life! Amen!!

The Trumpet Warning

Ezekiel 33:4-5 *'...then he who hears the sound of the trumpet and does not take warning, and a sword comes and takes him away, his blood will be on his own head. He heard the sound of the trumpet but did not take warning...'* (NASB)

Can you hear the warning sound of the trumpet?

Right now we are in the centre of a trumpet sound warning. 'Warning'= advanced notice of something. Most definitions give 'warning' as 'potential danger'. However, if we recognise the time we're in, we'll recognise that the warning is about the second coming of Christ our King, coming *'for to carry us home'*. The warning, although no different to that being given so many years ago, seems now more urgent as the time approaches.

However, in spite of the warnings, we have to ask whether we, God's ecclesia, truly believe that God is real. Although being given the word of God, His own word, as warnings, as reproof, many of us either act as if His word is not really true OR we parade as having no real fear of the AWESOME Almighty God. But, He is not to be mocked!

God is gracious, merciful and He understands our weaknesses. But this is not an excuse for us to ignore the warnings He gives about us getting right with Him, with each other. God sees the malice in our heart for each other. He sees the critical judgments we make about others. He sees the selfishness which drives us to hurt each other. He sees the greed for money, for position, for status which clouds our view of Him. But because of His unfailing love for us, He continues to sound the trumpet prompting us to take heed and get right for His arrival. And we continue to act as if He is not real.

Saints, GOD IS ALIVE and GOD IS REAL. He says it's not His desire that any should perish. Grace. So He continues to sound the trumpet.

So come on now Brothers and Sisters let us not be counted amongst those whose *'blood is upon his own head'* but let us turn and show reverential fear to the MOST HIGH GOD as we wait in preparedness as much as we can for our Bridegroom's return. Amen...Amen!

Enlarge My Territory

1 Chronicles 4:10 *'Now Jabez called on the Lord of Israel, saying, Oh that you would bless me indeed, and enlarge my border...And God granted him what he requested'.* (NASB)

Many of us have prayed this prayer of Jabez. It's a prayer that those who feel there's more, or who require more, would pray. Jabez's prayer is a well prayed prayer. But have you ever considered that while we're there praying for God to enlarge our coast/territory, that He may have already done so and is waiting for us to wake up, realise it and move in it? Have you considered that?

Jesus may be sitting on His throne waiting to give us directions of what we need to do in this enlarged space, but we are so limited in our view that we can't see we've already been enlarged. Oh oh! So we, in fact, become the obstacle to our own growth, delaying the instruction for the next step.

So although we have the territory, we're not stretching ourselves, reaching out our hands, taking that bigger step, cranking out our necks to see further because we don't recognise Jesus has sent the answer and so (help us Lord!) we remain stagnant! Wow! Instead, we keep praying "LORD, ENLARGE MY TERRITORY! ENLARGE MY TERRITORY and He's saying it's done, ENLARGE YOUR PERSPECTIVE!!

Wow! Doesn't the Word say if we ask anything according to His will, it shall be done? Doesn't the Word say that no good thing will He withhold from us? So come on now peeps! Stretch out your hands. Take those extra steps. You may well find where you thought the boundaries were, they are no longer there.

Amen!

Your Being Here is Not by Chance

Acts 17:26 *'...and He made from one man every nation of mankind to live on all the face of the earth, having determined their appointed times and the boundaries of their habitation'.* (NASB)

Do you ever sit down and consider why you were born in this era of the earth's existence and not say in the times of Abraham or Ruth, or even in the times of Queen Victoria or King George? Do you ever consider why you were born where you were born, and why you have ended up here in the country you are in now? You may have family members in other countries but you are where you are. Why were we born male or female? Why were we born into the race or culture that we are? Why?

This verse clearly tells us that it's all part of the Master's master plan. Each and every one of us has a unique purpose for being who we are, right where we are, right now! Oh yes, some of us would have loved to be living maybe in warmer climes, more exotic surroundings where the pressures of life are less. But at this point, at this time THIS is where the Master Planner desires for you to be. He has a plan and if we follow the leading of Holy Spirit in our lives, the plan unfolds.

The plan is that we manifest the Kingdom of God wherever we are positioned RIGHT NOW! Isaiah 61:1-3 tells us what that manifestation should look like - sharing the Gospel, bringing hope to the hopeless, bringing light to dark places, replacing sorrow with joy. THAT'S what we are supposed to be doing right where we are now at this appointed time.

Many say it's the greatest time to be alive in church history!! So let's just take a hold of who we are, where we are and do what needs to be done to advance the Kingdom. Let's thank God as we yield ourselves to Him to use us as He predestined.

Amen!

The Power of the Word

John 1: 1-4 *'In the beginning was the Word...He was in the beginning with God. All things came into being through Him and apart from Him nothing came into being that has come into being. In Him was life...'* (NASB)

This is such a powerful passage of scripture with so much depth and treasure. Some definitions of '**word**' include *'name'*, *'expression'*, *'appellation'*, *'instruction'*, *'order'*, *'command'*. The 'word' can be expressed as something written or spoken. It is used to formulate something. People often use phrases such as "Word!" when something powerful has been said. But John gives us insight into the original and first "WORD" – the "WORD" of God.

Imagine...the Ancient of Days saw that life needed to come upon the earth and so He opened His mouth and out of it came the "WORD" which contained life to create all things. The "WORD" was the fullest expression of God's power. The "WORD" came forth with instruction, bringing forth order by commanding things to get into line. Wow!! That same "WORD" has been expressed in writing just for us. That same expression of God's power, the "WORD" dwells in us. Now 'selah' that for a moment!

Can we even imagine if we really grasped the power that dwells in us enough to open our mouths and speak the "WORD" forth into our atmosphere, what we could create? Instead of moaning, grumbling, gossiping, slandering, putting others down, can you imagine what we could really bring into existence, if we access and use as we should the "WORD"???

Yahweh opened His mouth, brought forth the "WORD" and look at the outcome.

Saints, take heed.

Amen!!

The Shaken vs The Unshakeable

Hebrews 12: 28 *"Therefore since we receive a Kingdom which cannot be shaken, let us show gratitude, by which we may offer to God an acceptable service with reverence and awe;"* (NASB)

Saints of God, all around us now we are seeing some of the most fundamental institutions of this British nation lose their grip. Decisions made have affected the financial and property markets, businesses are in fear, house-owners are worried and to top it all up, those who are governing us have imploded and turned against themselves. What was once thought as stable has in a short space of time become unstable. Every day the media brings a new headline which plunges this nation further into despair about its future.

But as people of God we are not to forget that our God, who is Sovereign, sits above the circle of the Earth and is in total control. He has all power to blow on the things of this earth and they wither away. None of this was a shock to Him. It's His plans and purposes that are taking place no matter how adverse they look, how confusing they feel, how uncertain it all may seem. If we truly acknowledge and recognise the truth of who our God is, we will accept that nothing is uncertain with Yahweh. Every day we awake is a day closer to that Day when we as the righteous nation will enter into the City that He has built for us, a City that cannot be shaken, a strong City where the Lord Himself will be the government ruling with righteousness, justice and peace. And He wants for us all to enter.

Saints more than ever now, we need to really check ourselves, put down those things that we know are sinful and really get serious about our walk with, and worship of, the Almighty God. He is the only One who can guarantee us any stability. He is our solid Rock, our sure Foundation. He is the only One in whom we can safely place our trust. And He promises us that if we keep our minds on Him, He will keep us in perfect peace even in the midst of all the turmoil around us.

So come on Saints, let's show gratitude to our God for the unshakeable Kingdom He is giving us. Let's worship Him, honour him with reverence and awe, offering to him our acceptable service, Amen

Do You Know How Valuable You Are??

Matthew 6:26 *'Look at the birds of the air, that they do not sow nor reap nor gather into barns; yet your heavenly Father feeds them. Are you not worth much more than they?'* (NASB)

Do you know how valuable you are? Just think!

Your Father in heaven imagined you with all your specific character traits and physical measurements even before your bloodline started in Adam and Eve. He planned what role you'd hold in His kingdom while you were still in His creative mind, with your physical make up perfect to fit the works He had prepared for you to do.

Whether good or bad, spiritually fruitful or not, He knew exactly why He placed you in that particular family group so you would add to and enhance them and be a light in the darkness to them. He knew exactly what dispensation, what era of time He would bring you forth, the time when your specific work needed to be carried out.

He's made you unique. Just as there is no other like Him, there is no other like you in all the earth. Unique! As He imagined you, He also set aside spiritual gifts, talents, blessings, favour, specifically designed just for you! He saw from the start that there would be a fight for your soul, so came off His throne, came down in the form of man and died an inhumane death JUST for you. He knew you couldn't make it back to Him without His specific help so He gave you your own infilling of His Holy Spirit to assist you. Do you not see why He loves you so very much? Why you are SPECIAL in His sight? Why you are VALUABLE to Him? Wow!

With this in mind let's remember and keep on remembering that NO GOOD THING WILL HE WITHHOLD from you. He created you. He knows what works best for you and with you. Remember you are more valuable than the birds of the air and THEY get all their needs met. How much more you?

What a Father we have!! Seriously! What a GOOD Father!! Bless His Name! Amen.

Watch Out, Watch Out! The Heart is About!

Jeremiah 17:9 *'The heart is more deceitful than all else…"* (NASB)

The Heart. Such a small organ but plays such a major role in our physical, emotional and spiritual existence. The Heart! Can't live without it, be careful how you live with it. The Heart. This small organ which can get us into such BIG trouble. Jeremiah recognised the heart as being deceitful – dishonest, misleading, fraudulent – and if we check it, that's exactly what the Heart is. The Heart will leap over our common sense, leap over our spirit and go off in its own direction if we don't keep it covered with the truth of God's Word.

The Heart will take us to some places without us even recognising that we were on a journey until we reach the destination, wake up and find that we are in the midst of trouble. The deception of the Heart can destroy lives, break friendships, and kill trust. The Heart can have us so tricked that the outcome can be devastation, even turmoil in our lives. The Heart. Solomon recognised that all the issues of life flows from out of the depths of our Heart.

Can you imagine being fooled by your own Heart? We're easy prey though because we got to live with our Heart every day.

The Heart. We MUST keep regular daily, hourly, minute-by-minute checks on it. Check its flow. What's going in. What's coming out. What's taking root there. The Heart. Give it to Jesus daily to do a deep spring-clean knowing that as the One who created the Heart in the first place, He is the only One who can truly create in us a clean Heart and He is the only One who can help us keep our Heart right with Him and with others, Amen!

So watch out! Watch out! Your Heart is about and it's waiting to draw you in. Selah!

Amen!

But What If He Doesn't

Daniel 3:17-18 *"If it be so, our God whom we serve is able to deliver us from the furnace of blazing fire and He will deliver us out of your hand, O King. But even if He does not..."* (NASB)

Right from the start, we have to know, trust and believe that the God that we serve, Alpha and Omega, has a plan and no matter what, His plans must come to pass. What we don't know is how God will execute His plan and how our lives events constitute to being part of His plan.

Sometimes, we can find ourselves right in the middle of a *'fiery furnace'* of our own. We may not even see the 'furnace' lighting up but we definitely know when the fire is blazing. We may go through similar trials, not knowing how God is going to work our situation out only trusting that He will.

But what if God doesn't? What if, after all the fasting, praying, coming together in agreement with other saints, what if God never heals your illness, never delivers you from that work situation, never brings restoration to that family dispute, never saves your unsaved, never gets you out of that financial situation?? What if God doesn't? GOD IS SOVEREIGN and He will do things exactly how He wants possibly NOT how we hoped. His ways and thoughts are higher than ours.

He might bring that sickness onto death. Would He still be God to you? That financial situation may get to the state of bankruptcy where you lose everything. Would He still be God to you? He may never make a way out of that situation. Would He still be God to you? That family member may never accept Him. Would He still be God to you?

The three Hebrew boys made up their minds that even if God doesn't deliver them they would serve no other God. If God doesn't come through the way that you want, will you still worship Him? That's a question only you can answer but in considering it, we must know that we know that we know that regardless of the outcome, God still remains as God. He still remains as sovereign. His position never changes. Will yours?? Now that question, once again, is a 'Selah'!
Amen

Strength like No Other

2 Samuel 22:33 *'God is my strength and power and He makes my way perfect'*. (NKJV)

There probably has been no time like the present when we, the people of God really need to see and recognise Yahweh as our Strength. We're in the 11th hour; not approaching it or preparing for it, we are IN the 11th hour and Christ Jesus' second coming is upon us.

While we become more and more concerned about whether we are ready for the arrival of our Bridegroom, the enemy of our soul is becoming more and more anxious about his soon-to-be inevitable demise. And so he is waging war like never before. He's coming from every angle, with all types of assaults, insults, onslaughts physical, mental, emotional, financial and spiritual. BUT GOD!

Oh, thank God that we have a God who is alive, who has already assured us that we just need to draw close to Him, dwell in Him and He will give us the strength to get through all that comes at us. Oh, some of us feel that the battle is too heavy! Some of us feel that we can't go much further! Some of us feel we can't stand anymore!

Ah, but HE IS YOUR STRENGTH. The songwriter says *'Strength like no other'*. Almighty God does not get weary, He doesn't faint. He is not blind to what's going on! So lean on Him. Lean on His word. He knows you're weary but He says lean on Him, with prayer, with praise, with thanksgiving and He will carry you through to victory.

Ahh yes! He is our strength and our power and He has promised to make our way perfect in the way only He can.

Lean on Him.

Amen!

Don't Take Offence

Matthew 24:10-11 *'And at that time many will fall away and will betray one another and hate one another. Many false prophets will arise and will deceive many'.* (NASB)

It's so vital for our spiritual health that we don't allow offence to take root in our lives. When something 'takes root' that means its planted and ready to bear fruit.

Some definitions of 'offence' = *anger, resentment, indignation, exasperation, disgruntlement, animosity.* Not nice emotions. This verse shows us what the fruit of offence can look like.

Betrayal. We may feel so much indignation with a person that loyalty and love gets forgotten. We may do/say things against a person's character. If we don't put these feelings in check, confess them, our indignation may cause the fruit of hatred to grow. Remember the devil seeks who he may devour. If we give him a foothold he'll grab that fruit and multiply it.

Opening the door to offence is destructive. As we read through the verse, we read that many false prophets will rise up and deceive many.

But notice the succession. Offence comes in. Left to take root it bears fruit of betrayal and hatred. By the time hate comes in, we have moved so far from the word of God (which commands us to love) and given free rein to the spirit of deception to come and do whatever it wants in our lives.

And consider what that spirit of deception will do. Fill your head with lies about why you are offended, why you should stay offended, why you shouldn't forgive, why you are justified in speaking about that person, why no-one else should speak to that person. We may even get to the point where we don't even remember why we were offended in the first place! By that time the devil's laughing at the destruction he's caused.

You see Saints, why it's so important not to allow offence to even have a foothold?? Let us be a people who, when we feel that first sense of offence rearing its ugly head, we confess it, ask Daddy to help us move from it, forgive the one who brought it and keep on loving, Amen!

Do You Really Want What You Pray For??

Ephesians: 5:13 *'But when anything is exposed and reproved by the light, it is made visible and clear; and where everything is visible and clear, there is light'* (AMP).

The Bible say that God is working out His salvation in us. It say that He is faithful to complete the good work that He has started in us. The Word of God tells us that Almighty God knows our hearts. He knows much better than we ourselves of the things hidden within our hearts, some WE may not even know!

But we pray those prayers don't we..."Lord create in me a clean heart" "Lord search my heart and know me, see if there be any wicked way in me"? Ahhh, when we pray these types of prayers, we are effectively giving God permission (because you know our Father is a gentleman and won't force Himself on anyone) to deal with our hearts.

But Saints, be prepared because when YAHWEH starts to uncover and bring to the surface stuff that we have in the crevice of our heart, be prepared to do what He says for that 'clean heart' to be created. Isn't that what He requires of us??? Our hearts, totally and fully purified?

And so, as the verse says, when what is hidden becomes exposed, reproved, made visible and clear, there is light. Saints, isn't that what we want, for all darkness within us to have HIS light shone upon it?

Selah. Let's not resist.

Amen.

Don't You Recognise Me Anymore???

Hebrews 9:8 *'By this the Holy Spirit points out that the way into the (true Holy of) Holies is not yet thrown open as long as the former (the outer portion of the) tabernacle remains a recognised institution and is still standing.'* (AMP)

There is something very powerful about this verse if we can relate it to ourselves as tabernacles of God's Spirit. We know when we accept Christ, His Spirit comes and dwells in us. From then on, once we are in submission to His working out in us, the Holy Spirit will, over time, draw us closer to Christ, also making us more like Him.

However, it is possible for us to resist the Spirit's working out in us. It is possible for us ourselves to choose to hold onto things, habits, thought-patterns, mind-sets, attitudes of the old self to the point where others don't witness that much difference in our lives. It's possible for us to allow our 'former tabernacle' to 'remain' and to be 'still standing' as the 'recognised institution' in OUR lives. It's possible that by doing this WE hinder him from going there.

He desires to go there. Actually, it's in our best eternal interest to allow Him to go there so that He can do that deeper work in us that will get us looking, thinking and behaving more like our Saviour Christ Jesus. So let's examine ourselves. Do we recognise where we may be doing the above? Are we the ones who have 'not yet thrown open' the way and given access to Holy Spirit to get down into those deep places in our lives?

God is gracious.

Now is the time for us to put down our own institution; now is the time to allow ourselves to become unrecognisable to those around us so that they can recognise more clearly Christ in us and through us. We hear it so many times, but it's a true statement - We may be the only Bible a person reads. So let's allow His Spirit full access.

Amen!

Good Trees Can't Bear Bad Fruit

Genesis 15:13-14 *God said to Abram, Know for certain that your descendants will be strangers in a land that is not theirs where they will be enslaved and oppressed four hundred years. But I will also judge the nation whom they will serve and afterwards they will come out with many possessions'.* (NASB)

Being a parent is not an easy task. Being a Christian parent is even harder as our challenges are both physical and spiritual. Many of us have grown children not walking the way of The Lord Jesus. Maybe you raised them in church and becoming adults, they made choices to go their own way. Maybe some have never yet walked in The Way.

Jesus said that 'A good tree cannot bear bad fruit...' No matter what our children and their behaviour looks like now, they ARE NOT bad fruit because WE ARE good trees!! The children who are not walking God's way have been duped into becoming 'strangers in a land that is not their own'. Some of them may look comfy there, but deep in their souls they know something is amiss. But God allows (because without His ok, it cannot happen) our seed to dwell in the stranger's camp, eating out of the stranger's plate, take counsel from the stranger's mouth, because He, GOD, has a plan! A plan to bring Him glory! A plan the strangers could never comprehend.

We never know how, when or what it will look like when God does it. But when deliverance comes for the children and they are plucked out from the stranger's land...HALLELHUIA, they shall come out with 'great substance'! Great testimonies! Great power! Great turnaround HALLELHUIA!! And don't worry because God Himself will judge those who held our children captive, who afflicted them and caused them to serve them! Amen!

So parents, hold on tight if this is you. The end is not yet, not until we see our children returning back to their own land, serving the Lord God. Amen!

The Blood He Shed, He Sent Ahead

Hebrews 12:24 *'And to Jesus, the Mediator of a new covenant, and to the sprinkled blood which speaks better than the blood of Abel'.* (NASB)

How can we ever comprehend with our natural minds, what Yahweh did, when in His infinite wisdom He put in that blood of His Son a power so great that it has been able to transcend throughout time to meet us in the 21st century and not have lost one ounce of its power???

How can we ever make sense of the fact that that blood which dripped from our Saviour's body as He made His way to Calvary, as He was wounded, pierced, chastised, nailed to the cross, that blood that dripped from Him, how can we ever understand that it's THAT SAME BLOOD which today offers us protection against demonic forces, casts down strongholds, releases captives, heals the sick, purifies environments, pierces through the spirit realm and so much more?? That precious blood looked ahead in time and saw you and I and knew that if it wasn't shed, we wouldn't stand a chance.

That blood! Our propitiation! That blood! It sanctifies our souls. He exchanged that blood for our souls and then gave us authority to sprinkle the Blood ourselves, by faith and declaration, whenever we need to. That blood!

Nothing has ever matched it. Nothing ever will! Don't take it for joke. It's too precious to play games with. Don't leave it behind. It's too necessary to be left unused. Don't stop being amazed by its power. It's too dynamic to be restricted!!

So, each time we recall and celebrate His death and resurrection, REJOICE as much in the POWER of HIS BLOOD.

Amen!!

The Youths Are Our Responsibility!!

Psalm 144:12 *'Let our sons in their youth be as grown up plants, and our daughters as corner pillars fashioned as for a palace'.* (NASB)

Saints, whether you are biological parents or not, every one of us has a responsibility for the young people of our society. Whether they know Christ or not (yet) we, men and women of God have the mandate to stand in the gap for them. If truth be told, we're sleeping as a church in relation to this.

Every day a youth gets stabbed, loses their lives. Families divide as young people face prison or sink deeper into drug use. Every day, our young women are being sexually exploited or are part of the plan to exploit other females. Satan ain't resting! While we the church are being jealous of each other's gifts and ministries, while we act with each other worse than non-believers act, while we're being too busy supposedly 'doing for God', Satan is snuffing our young people out under our noses. Those he hasn't killed, he is luring further away from 'life' in Christ and closer to a hopeless future.

Saints we have got to declare the Word of The Lord over their lives, know that it is sharper than any two edged sword and can change hearts! Declaring the word over them will bring release, deliverance, freedom and will propel them into their destiny.

Saints they can't do this without you and me because they don't know how to. We need to be declaring who they are in Christ even when they don't look that way. If we declare it long enough, with faith, we will see it come to pass.

It's us! It's down to us. We, the Church, have the authority from above to turn young lives around. What are we going to do with that authority? It's your call! Amen!

Jesus, Our Sure and Steadfast Hope

Hebrews 6:19 '*This hope we have as an anchor of the soul, a hope both sure and steadfast and one which enters within the veil...*' (NASB)

People of God, even if it's just for the moments you spend reading this "WORD" Up encouragement today, just take a minute and give some 'Selah' (pause and think about that) time to the unchangeable truth which is that we have a hope in Christ Jesus upon which our soul is anchored!! Wow! The words of the song says "I am so blessed, my soul is at rest, Oh Lord I give You thanks". What an assurance!! What a guarantee!!

When the hospitals can't guarantee hope, we have Jesus. When the job can't guarantee hope, we have Jesus. When the security forces can't guarantee hope, we have Jesus. When the financial system can't guarantee hope, we have Jesus. When the family system can't guarantee hope, we have Jesus. When the education system can't guarantee hope, we have Jesus!

The amplified Bible says it like this *'Now we have this hope as a sure and steadfast anchor of the soul (it cannot slip and it cannot break down under whoever steps out upon it - a hope) that reaches farther and enters into (the very certainty of the Presence) within the veil*. My My My!

When people say they lose hope, they really do not know the HOPE upon which they stand, if they belong to Christ. This should even push us more to pray for the unsaved because what hope do they have when they know not the LORD???

He is our SURE FOUNDATION and will NEVER BREAK DOWN no matter what type of weight we stand upon Him with. So Saints PRAISE JESUS TODAY HALLEHUIA, and remember that with Him NOTHING IS HOPELESS, Amen!

Recognise the Idols in Your Heart

Ezekiel 14:2-3 *'And the word of the LORD came to me, saying, ³ "Son of man, these men have set up their idols in their hearts, and put before them that which causes them to stumble into iniquity. Should I let Myself be inquired of at all by them?* (NASB)

Wow!! As Christians we too can have idols hidden deep in our hearts. Definition of idol is something or someone placed higher than God. Idols could be money, pleasure, unforgiveness, bitterness, jealousy, pride, a person, a job, a thing. Whatever it is, it's an idol, something that we don't want to give up.

Sometimes idols are not seen to the human eye. But God, who sees the deeper things of the heart, sees them. And imagine, God can allow us to be deceived through prophetic voices when we seek them, not through a pure heart, but through the idols of our heart!! Wow! That's deep! So we can actually be led on a totally wrong path through the word given by a prophet because we have kept an idol as first place in our heart! Oh my!

That's why we need to constantly check our heart, really seeking God to expose the hidden things in our heart. We need to forgive quickly, seek forgiveness regularly, check ourselves for pride, and check if we are placing anything before God, even that which appears to be godly.

This is serious stuff! Wow! Both spiritually and physically, it's important to keep the heart healthy Amen, as the last thing we want is to receive a false prophecy that sends us in the wrong direction. THAT will be detrimental to our "health" in all aspects.

Let's take time today to do an honest reality check. And let's not be fooled. Remember God is all seeing, all knowing,

Amen!

Living as a Doer

Romans 2:13 *'For it is not the hearers of the Law who are just before God, but the doers of the Law will be justified'.* (NASB)

Most of us Christians can testify that we know at least a handful of scripture verses which we can recite and pull out when needed. Those who have been followers of Christ for a long time may even be able to quote chapter and verse. The Word of God in our toolbox is the most effective piece of equipment we will ever need.

Father God instructs us to be diligent students of the word so that we can be approved by Him. So we recite scripture and study the word. But the greatest requirement is that we actually DO what the word says.

Let's not deceive ourselves and think that as long as we know and study the word, we are ok. We know and study the word but we still gossip and slander. We know and study the word but we still harbor ill thoughts in our hearts. We know and study the word but we still judge others for doing and not doing the things which we ourselves do and do not do! We know and study the word but do we really walk in love? Really? Wow!! Doesn't the word say that God will not be mocked?? Lord God help us!

How much do we really submit and yield ourselves to the power of the living and active word of God, allowing it to pierce through to our soul and spirit so that we naturally live it? That's what God wants. He wants us, His people, to LIVE His word, LIVE His commands and we can only do that if we truly yield our whole being, whole heart, whole life to His word.

Hard task?? Yes and our gracious God knows that. Impossible? No, because with God nothing is impossible.

So Saints, let's take the measuring stick off others and check ourselves remembering it's the 'doers' of the Law who will be justified.

Amen!

It's Yours. God said it!!

Deuteronomy 2:24 *"Arise, set out and pass through the valley of Amon. Look! I have given Sihon the Amorite, King of Hesbon and his land into your hand; begin to take possession and contend with him in battle'.* (NASB)

Wow!! Sihon represented an obstacle which stood in the way of the Israelites moving forward. What stands in YOUR way of moving forward? But Moses, led by the Spirit of the Lord, had already declared that the Israelites were going to possess Sihon's land. So in this verse the Lord instructs the Israelites to '*possess*' the land and to '*contend*' with Sihon. How much more confidence can we have than when the Lord God Himself tells us to contend with something and possess it because He's already put in our hands??

'contend' means to struggle or exert oneself to obtain or retain possession of... What has the Lord told you is yours?? Whatever it is be it healing, your new home, a spouse, salvation for your unsaved, financial provision, that degree, that job, that ministry, whatever it is that He has said is yours, He has already put it in your hands and He's saying 'CONTEND' for it, 'CONTEND' for it!! You know you're going to have to CONTEND for it because the devil isn't going to want to give it up. He's been holding onto that thing for so long now that he believes it's his. He believes that he owns it. He's even managed to fool some of us into thinking we shouldn't bother about that thing as it's his! LIAR! But Lord God says 'BEGIN TO POSSESS IT AND CONTEND' for it belongs to you!!

The Israelites could not lose. Why? Because they had the Almighty Jehovah behind them. Saints neither can you lose for you have the Almighty Jehovah behind you! Don't watch how long you been contending for. Don't even be swayed by the severity of the struggle. If the Lord God has said it's yours, go possess it! Amen!! Contend for it and possess it. Give Him thanks and ask Him for the strength and strategy to endure until you overcome that Amorite standing in your way, Amen! Sometimes we have to contend and struggle because there is something in the process that will take us to the next level, but the Lord said possess it and contend for it because he has already declared its yours!! Amen!!!

Prune Me Lord, Prune Me!

John 15:2 *"Any branch in me that does not bear fruit (that stops bearing) He cuts away (trims off, takes away) and He cleanses and repeatedly prunes every branch that continues to bear fruit, to make it bear more and richer and more excellent fruit".* (AMP)

Walking in submission to God gives Jesus the go-ahead to go way down in our lives and pull out some stuff! Stuff that's laid dormant, stuff we aren't aware of, stuff we've forgotten about, stuff we've buried, stuff we thought we'd dealt with, STUFF!

Some stuff is so deep, so old, it's grown roots and entwined itself in our lives until it looks and feels like it's part of us. Some stuff we've pressed down so far it's actually grown moldy and stinks but we can't smell it because it's become a familiar smell to us. Smells like us.

But know that 'stuff' hinders our growth just like unwanted thistle. So Jesus chooses His time to get down to business in us and to start pulling that stuff out. Wow! That's if we allow Him to.

Pulling up roots is a task! It's unnerving. It's messy. It dis-lodges things around it. Once pulled up, whatever that stale thing was it was feeding dies. But, if the Lord is doing a works then so be it!

Know that The Living Water won't leave you dry. The Potter won't leave you un-moulded. The Great Physician won't leave you unhealed. The Comforter won't leave you alone and the Restorer won't leave you incomplete. Christ prunes us so we can bring God more glory, Amen!

So come on Saints! Going through some pruning??? Give God praise!! Praise Him for the 'pruning' because the verse says that 'He...repeatedly prunes every branch that continues to bear fruit, to make it bear more and richer and more excellent fruit,

Amen!

Be On Your Guard

Galatians 2:4 *But it was because of the false brethren secretly brought in, who had sneaked in to spy out our liberty which we have in Christ Jesus, in order to bring us into bondage.* (NASB)

Saints, we got to be on our guard. It's not everyone who comes to us proclaiming 'Jesus' who have the true Spirit of the Lord as a guarantee living in them. In this day when it's even possible that the elect will be deceived, we got to ensure that we have activated the gift of discernment we have, which if we listen carefully to, will alert us that something isn't quite right.

Oh, don't be fooled, they will pursue you saying 'love is perseverance' but be on guard, for as much as they look like disciples of Jesus and speak like disciples of Jesus, they have been sent through the back door for one thing and one thing only... to slowly but surely bring you down. They will bring what sounds so close to gospel truth. Their 'light' will seem to shine so brightly but be on the alert!! Holy Spirit within you will start sounding alarm bells that something isn't right. Saints, heed those bells! Go no further for the more we listen and get drawn in to this 'other gospel' is the further we will be taken from the truth and the deeper we will be brought into bondage.

That's the devil's plan is it not? He IS the deceiver, who comes like an angel of light is he not? Saints, be not deceived or drawn in. Let the true gospel of Jesus Christ reign in your heart always. The Word of God says *'resist the devil and he shall flee*' (James 4:7)!

Amen!

Be Strong!

2 Timothy 2:1 *'So you, my son, be strong (constantly strengthened) and empowered in the grace that is (to be found only) in Christ Jesus'.* (AMP)

Well, the REAL testing of our faith is definitely in motion. If there was ever a time that the people of God needed to pray for strength, its now!

There's been a slow and steady change of climate in the spiritual atmosphere which, really, is no longer slow. If we are discerning, we'll see that things are moving at an accelerated rate. There is an intensity of evil and wickedness covering the earth; killings, violence, wars, various types of atrocities, various types of confusion be it sexual or mental. It's all in our face. The systems in our infrastructure are crumbling, failing, becoming rapidly unrecognisable. But in all of this, the people of God, us, who are called by His name are being instructed to be strong in the grace found ONLY in Christ Jesus.

In Christ alone can we stand firm. In Christ alone can we have the strength to endure not only what is here now but what is to come. In Christ alone can we find the strength we need to pray and intercede for this world. In Christ alone will we have the strength to remain steadfast, immovable able to continue to give ourselves to the work of the Lord, knowing that if we endure there is a great reward.

Colossians 1:23 says *'if indeed you continue in the faith grounded and steadfast...'* We can only do that by the strength found in Jesus. We must pray for strength, daily!!! Saints, our enemy searches the earth seeking who he may devour. We need strength or else we'll go under!!

So, today, pray for strength, not just for yourself but for the body of Christ worldwide. Pray that as we abide under the shadow of the Almighty, that He strengthens us and strengthens us and strengthens us, Amen! We can only endure this race if we are strong in the Lord and in the power of HIS might. Glory to God!!! I pray for you, that you be strong in Christ Jesus, Amen!!!

What's That You're Saying?

Luke 24:15 *'While they were talking and discussing, Jesus Himself approached and began travelling with them;'* (NASB)

Would your conversation be inviting to Jesus? Would He feel welcomed to join in your conversation? Is God pleased when you open your mouth?

Our Father in heaven loves to hear us talk about Him. It gives Jesus great pleasure to hear us exalting Him, praising Him speaking of His wondrous acts, bringing glory to His name. When we do this we stir up an atmosphere of praise wherever we are and the Spirit of the Lord shows up!

In His showing up, He'll bring revelation, He'll bring a word of prophecy, or even a word of wisdom. He'll bring deliverance, a refreshing, and an awakening of the Spirit within us.

The Psalmist says *'let the words of my mouth...be acceptable in your sight* (Psalm 19:14). As people of God, as those who have reverential fear for Him, our No1 goal in life should be to please Him and this means within our conversations also.

So...what is it you were saying last night? Or yesterday? Was it welcoming to Jesus? Remember He is always listening. Selah...

Amen.

What Are You Bringing?

1 Corinthians 14:26 *'...When you assemble each one has a psalm, has a teaching, has a revelation, has a tongue, has an interpretation...'* (NASB)

Generally people come to the house of God with the expectation of receiving something from Him through the Pastor, Priest, Bishop or whoever the preacher is . People come expecting a blessing, healing, a word, something. We may even get a little 'disappointed' if we don't 'feel' we received during the service.

But this word clearly tells us that we are the ones who should be coming with something when we assemble together. We should be so stirred for God that we come just bursting to pour out something into the congregation, more importantly to join others in pouring out blessings and thanksgiving, ministering onto the One who saved us, Jesus Christ the King.

Bringing a psalm could lift someone's countenance. A word of teaching could edify another. A revelation could bring clarity or direction to someone's situation. An interpretation could change the course of another's life. We should come together to strengthen and encourage each other, remind each other of who God is!

So ask God what He will have you bring next time you join with other believers. Don't always come to receive but be filled with the Spirit to the point of overflow and come willing to pour out.

Amen!

Strange Instruction

2 Kings 4:3 *'Then he said, 'Go borrow vessels at large for yourself from all your neighbours, even empty vessels; do not get a few.'* (NASB)

Watch out for strange instructions as God prepares you for increase. This widow had no idea why she was told to go borrow as many vessels as she could, no idea that God was about to bring the kind of supernatural increase to that ONE jar of oil which she would be able to sell and make enough money to pay her way out of debt. But she obeyed the instruction given and God made provision exceedingly and abundantly for her.

Some of us may have already received our instruction but are sitting on it, for whatever reason. We're not only sinning in disobedience but are missing out on our increase as well. Remember the God we serve owns the thousand cattle upon the hill. He has riches in glory. He is the giver of all good things. So whatever He has in store for us, His children, will always be good.

So watch out for strange instruction. Pray about the instruction given and even if you don't quite get it, remember the Father's ways are higher than our ways, His thoughts higher than out thoughts. Who can understand Him?

Just be obedient, follow instruction and be prepared to receive.

Amen.

Thank God for My Afflictions

Genesis 41:52 *"...For" he said "God has made me fruitful in the land of my affliction."* (NASB)

The Word says that our steps are ordered by the Lord. It says He guides our paths so we must recognise that we are God-led to both rocky places as well as to smooth roads, each for a reason or a season.

Sorry to say this Saints but 'affliction' is our portion. God warns us that we will definitely have experiences of afflictions on our journey. But know that Father does nothing without purpose where His greater plans for us are concerned. We very rarely take notice of what God is doing IN us through difficult times. We rarely notice changes He is making IN us until someone points it out or until we are faced with situations and realise we deal differently with them. Sometimes we'll face the same situation until changes He desires in us takes place.

Pruning is painful with the pain being more evident than the fruit being produced in the pain. But remember, God is the One ordering our steps. So be encouraged Child of God. When going through affliction, no matter the type, intensity or source, just say "Father, thank You for the fruits being produced in me at this time".

Amen!

Wait Patiently

Psalm 37: 7 *"Rest in the LORD and wait patiently for Him;"* (NASB)

Walking with Christ Jesus brings assurance that He will take care of all things related to us. At times we feel we need to be running around fixing things, trying to changing people but that's not it! Christ says rest and wait patiently for Him.

That's not easy when there's something, someone we want and we want it now! It's not easy when we feel someone needs changing and we want them to change now! It's not easy when we're in the midst of a crisis and we want resolve now! The key word is 'patiently' meaning 'calmly enduring'. That's not easy. But the Bible says that all good things come from God. It also says that no good thing will He withhold from the upright.

So, let's quit trying to sort things for ourselves. Instead let's wait patiently for God being assured that whatever He brings, whenever it comes, it will be excellent! After all when patience has been perfected, James 1:4 say we will lack nothing.

Amen!

Mind Control

Psalm 145:5 *'On the glorious splendor of your majesty and on your wonderful works, I will meditate'.* (NASB)

It is so easy to allow our minds to run away with all kinds of thoughts of worry, thoughts of concern. In this day, so much goes on in the world which, if we allow it, could consume our minds completely. Issues within our personal lives which again, if we allow them, could haunt our minds from dusk till dawn.

But this verse reminds us exactly what we should be meditating on - *the glorious splendor of God's majesty and His wonderful works.* WOW!

With this on our minds, no matter what is happening around us, to us, we will continue to smile and shine for Jesus Christ. Society will be perturbed as to how you manage to smile in the midst of its turmoil. Your enemies, those you know and those you don't, will wonder how you manage to still be at peace even while they try their best to bring you down.

Remember, Peter only began to sink when he took his eyes off of Jesus as they walked on water! So, from today, let your focus and your meditation be only on the GREAT and AWESOME LORD GOD and point those who try to distract you in His direction.

Amen!

Time for Change

Isaiah 9:2 *'The people who walk in darkness will see a great light; those who live in a dark land, the light will shine on them'.* (NASB)

Today, we see the bringing in of a new leader and leadership over this country. We have to know and trust that this is God's plan. As Christians we have a mandate to pray for our leaders, pray for our nation because God says that this is how we shall live a peaceable life. Remember back in Genesis the Lord God gave man dominion to rule over all the earth. That was lost for a while after the fall, but in Christ Jesus we again have authority, as the people of God, over the Earth. If we could only just truly believe that, not as individuals and groups here and there, but as the unified Body of Christ, we would see the hand of the Father at work mightily.

With this new leadership coming in, we need to arise and really pray pray pray for this nation, for its leaders. We want to see leaders who are submitted to the leadership of Christ Jesus. We want leaders who will not compromise the statutes of God. We want to see a new thing done in this land where righteousness and justice is central. We want to see our nation healed and families restored. We want to see that covenant of death over our nation broken. We want to see souls running to Christ and we want to see this nation saved. We want the Light of the world to shine in this nation, shine into the dark places and to bring new light and new hope to this land.

People of God, no other group of people have the backing of the Almighty God but us. No other group of people have the Spirit of the Living God dwelling in them but us!

So let's pray without ceasing and allow God's will to be done in this nation through us as we make a new commitment to be united as nothing else will suffice and even more than that, the eternal lives of others depends on our unity Amen, Amen!

Inspired By His Word

End of Part One...

Sadly, you have come to the end of the first edition of Inspired By His Word. Did you enjoy what you read? Were you blessed? God's word is lovely isn't it?? If you've enjoyed them, then I'd like to encourage you to look out for the second installment. It's on its way.

If you've been blessed by this publication bless someone else with a copy. This is a fabulous gift for all year round and can be read over and over again and still be relevant. I think the phrase is '*timeless*'.

Relationship not Religion

If you don't know Christ as your personal Lord and Saviour and would like to develop a relationship with Him, He would love that. He's been waiting for you since time began. It's about trading the old life for the new, being born again, no more worrying about what happens to you when you die.

Want that...? Then say the prayer of Salvation which follows, from your heart and Christ will hear. You may not feel anything different, but it's a walk of faith, just believing in your heart. Once you've done that, tell someone who knows Christ, find a good Bible believing Church and start your walk with God.

You won't regret it, trust me! The walk with Christ, although not always easy, is definitely always amazing!!

Prayer of Salvation

Dear God,

Because of what Adam and Eve did in the Garden of Eden, I can only come to you now as a sinner seeking your forgiveness for every sin in my life. I believe that Jesus Christ died in my place, giving His life on the Cross of Calvary paying the price for all my past, present and future sins.

I am willing right now to turn from this life of sin, of doing things my way, and accept Jesus Christ as my personal Lord and Saviour. I commit myself to You putting my life in Your hands and ask You to send the Holy Spirit into my life, to fill me and take control and allow me to be the person You have always meant for me to be.

I believe that by faith, I am now a new creation who desires to follow Jesus Christ for the rest of my life.

Thank you Almighty God for always loving me even when I didn't know you did.

In Jesus Name I pray
Amen

Welcome. You are now a member of the household of God. Angels in heaven are rejoicing that you have come back home where you rightly belong. Amen!!

Now, find someone who also believes in the Lord Jesus Christ and tell them that you have accepted Christ. This is your testimony. Once you've done that find a really good Bible believing Church that lives and promotes the truth of God's word and get yourself plugged in!

This is the exciting start of the rest of your life.

God bless you.

Final Word For Now...

Look out for '***Inspired By His Word***' Volume 2.
It's on its way.

Blessings All
Mary

ABOUT THE AUTHOR

Mary Hilton was born in England in 1964 to parents Kenneth and Veronica Hilton, both now sadly deceased. Mary, the second youngest of 8 siblings was raised in the east end of London, where she has lived all her life.

Mary is a qualified Social Worker who has a background in working with young people from all walks of life. She is passionate about issues which affect young people. As a result of her passion, Mary founded and established the Praying Parents Group back in 2015 which meets monthly to pray about the needs of children and young people and for their salvation.

Mary is also a Poetic Minister whose poems are greatly influenced by her experiences as a Christian. She has shared her work in various forums and has touched many with the anointed and powerful words which stem from the Word of God.

Mary's passion is to see people of God operating at full capacity in His Kingdom. As an encourager, she seeks to bring joy, strength and encouragement to others through her ministry Christ Inspired Words Ministry.

Inspired By His Word

Printed in Great Britain
by Amazon